#1nspiring™

Praise for *#1nspiring*

"Everyone runs around with a lot of ideas, but you only need one spark to ignite your idea and start to make a product from it—and that's what *#1nspiring* can do for you."
Marc Wesselink, Partner, VentureRock

"*#1nspiring* helps you think about your ideas and convert them into a realistic business plan. The A1 inspiration canvas makes it easier to define your business goals and strategy, and with help from the coaches and other attendants, you create a realistic action plan within a day."
Annette Beerepoot, Innovation consultant

"Take your business plan to the next level in one day. Together with experts and mentors, we'll inspire you and explain how to successfully plan your business."
Erik Broekhuijsen, Growth expert and mentor

"Remember, there is no recipe book for life! There are no right or wrong pieces of advice. In the end, we all make our choices, and the person looking in the mirror is the only one we can point our finger at. The happiness of that person depends on you. Be free, listen carefully, but chart your own way to love, happiness, and success in life. Say 'yes' and let your heart guide you; you will be amazed and impressed."
Amir Sabirović, CEO, Digital Savages

"It is like Walt Disney said: 'The way to get started is to quit talking and begin doing.' That's *#1nspiring* to me: learning by doing."

Michel Ariens, Founder, Yourcrew.online

"*#1nspiring* is a great tool that will help you take the first steps in developing and testing your idea. Entrepreneurs do not have to spend valuable time studying theories of business model development—this tool is both inspiring and easy to use."

Dženan Šarić, Director,
Startup Studio of the Mozaik Foundation

"As an entrepreneur, you can do with some inspiration every now and then. *#1nspiring* is the perfect place to find it. It gave me the opportunity to talk to the people who are 'getting there,' as well as the people who 'already got there,' so you can learn from both parties. The guidance from the coaches is especially useful, because their experience can shed some light on some of your problems as well as help you learn to keep things simple. Why are you doing what you are doing, who is it for, and what problems are you solving for your customers? Valuable lessons on a very inspiring day!"

Muriel Horst, Managing partner, Equs Film

"*#1nspiring* is a place for you to translate your ideas into a map of actions. An eye-opening session that will propel you to do amazing things."

Marta Blocka, Co-founder, Mentalist

"Learn to create your own map for the future."

Arne van Oosterom, Co-founder, Design Thinkers Group and Founder, Future Skills Academy

"I fell in love with the #1nspiring method. In a simple but smart way, you will get high-quality training in a short amount of time. *#1nspiring* will inspire you and equip you with the necessary knowledge to help you make your dream come true."

Minela Zerdo-Puljić, Founder, OKRUGLA Kocka

"I love to compare the #1nspiring approach with LEGO: Start building your basis, the inspiration canvas, with DUPLO. Sharpen your value proposition and business model canvas with LEGO. Continue to build, measure, and learn like the best lean startups with TECHNICAL LEGO. All the parts fit together, and help you to grow your entrepreneurial success."

André Bolland, Innovation expert and teacher entrepreneurship

"*#1nspiring* provides the entrepreneur an overview of the current state of their company. But more important, it provides clear building blocks that help form concrete steps into moving the company to the next phase."

Pieter Christiaan Vermeer, Partner, INVESTOR ready

"The mediocre teacher tells. The good teacher explains. The superior teacher demonstrates. The great teacher inspires. The name *#1nspiring* says it all. Be inspired."

Jin Han, Investor and mentor, Globus International

"*#1nspiring* is a fast and easy way to start a business. It is organized and structured as a business canvas."

Jaime San Martin, Business development, Atlann

"*#1nspiring* comes with an easy-to-learn approach based on the fundamental knowledge as a strong background. You want to do it, because it is fun! And every business, no matter how long its history, can be filled with new ideas end energy. Sometimes it just needs an #1nspiring spark."

Maciej Kupisiewicz, Founder Olgroup Multimedia

"Meaningful businesses grow by growing people. *#1nspiring* helps you and your partners grow."

Ingrid van Rossum, Co-founder, Fuenta

"'Hocus, pocus, focus' is what *#1nspiring* said and my business plan was ready to be read. Blessed with new ideas and moving forward. *#1nspiring* inspired me to help others to get their business groove on."

Salina Chisholm, Small business entrepreneur and coach, Lab of Purpose

"Inspiration is the water that feeds the plant, which is called motivation. *#1nspiring* ensures that you are using high-quality water."

Josuel Rogers, Motivator and coach

"*#1nspiring* moves you forward. As long as you are open to new opportunities, anything is possible."

Iris Versluis, Small business owner, CyanIris

"Read *#1nspiring* and explore for yourself a way up."

Erwin Kenter, Founder, There

YOUR NEXT STEP IN
BUSINESS
DEVELOPMENT

TRANSFORMING
IDEAS
INTO REALITY

Bart
Jenezon

NEW YORK

LONDON • NASHVILLE • MELBOURNE • VANCOUVER

#1nspiring™

Your Next Step in Business Development

Published in New York, New York, by Morgan James Publishing. Morgan James is a trademark of Morgan James, LLC. www.MorganJamesPublishing.com

Proudly distributed by Ingram Publisher Services.

Morgan James BOGO™

A **FREE** ebook edition is available for you or a friend with the purchase of this print book.

CLEARLY SIGN YOUR NAME ABOVE

Instructions to claim your free ebook edition:
1. Visit MorganJamesBOGO.com
2. Sign your name CLEARLY in the space above
3. Complete the form and submit a photo of this entire page
4. You or your friend can download the ebook to your preferred device

ISBN 9781631954832 paperback
ISBN 9781631954856 ebook
Library of Congress Control Number:
2021900089

Original Design:
Alex Venneker
www.vennekerdesign.com

Cover & Interior Design by:
Christopher Kirk
www.GFSstudio.com

Editor:
Tracy Brown-Hamilton

Morgan James PUBLISHING Builds **with... Habitat for Humanity®** Peninsula and Greater Williamsburg

Morgan James is a proud partner of Habitat for Humanity Peninsula and Greater Williamsburg. Partners in building since 2006.

Get involved today! Visit
MorganJamesPublishing.com/giving-back

Acknowledgments

Milan Kusmuk, Pavel Cholakov, Franziska Drinkler, Margot Reesink, Jolanta van Holstein, Matias Moreno, Robbert Roelofsen, Diederik Schuitemaker, Bram van der Boon, Claudia Deken, Chris Shakison, Jennifer Waller, Basant Marhe, Amir Sabirović, Arne van Oosterom, Frank Brouwer, Michel Ariens, Dzenan Saric, Annette Beerepoot, Zoran Puljić, Eddie Custovic, Pieter Christiaan Vermeer, Pieter Vermeer, Salina Chisholm, Iris Versluis, Sicco Bijzen, Angéla van Zelst, Mark de Jong, Danny Willemse, Franklin Warning, Marlies Gabriel, Marita Stuart-Schoonderwoerd, Naomi van der Burgt, Sonia Bagga, Willy Pardijs, Freek van Wensen, Lisette Winkel-Hendrikse, Kalle Palomaki, Anna C. Mallon, Erwin Kenter, Menno Weij, Ernst Hoestra, Matthijs Kat, Robert van Dortmond, Eduard Schaepman, Sylvia Bakker, Jaime San Martin, Zagros Ardalan, Judith Smits, Robert-Jan van Zessen, Richard Manuel, Anna Willems, Eveline Smeets, Richard Reese, Richard Henderickx, Gerben van der Werf, Cesar Sierhuis, Frits van Noortwijk, Ronald Panis, Patrick Gouka, Piet Hein van der Kroon, Teun van der Vorm, Muriel Horst, Marta Blocka, Andreea Stegarescu, Willem Gunzeln, Rutger de Hamer, Mirjam Schram, Ingrid van Rossum, Geert-Jan Beekman, Michel Arends, Sandra Brouwer, John Smith, Adrie Reinders, Roeland Reinders, Ben Valks, David Velt, Thierry de Vries, Bert Dijkshoorn,

Ted Munter, Frenz van de Grift, Erica Blankestijn, Jan Oostenbrink, Marian van de Meer, Karolin Kruiskamp, Pauline Siebers, Johan Steenkamp, Vince Balk, Vicky Fasten, Freek van Amelsvoort, Eric Eggink, Hugo Clercx, Zoran van Gessel and many others.

Special Support

Nina Elias, André Bolland, Josuel Rogers, Isabel Hamer, Minela Zerdo-Puljić, Maria Lucia Bermudez, Marcel Belt, Jin Han, Pieter de Haes, Maciej Kupisiewicz, Rob van de Meer, Carolin Hornbach, Serghei Ghidora, Michiel Janssen, Erik Broekhuijsen, and Marc Wesselink.

Thank you for your inspiration.

Table of Contents

"Practice makes perfect"

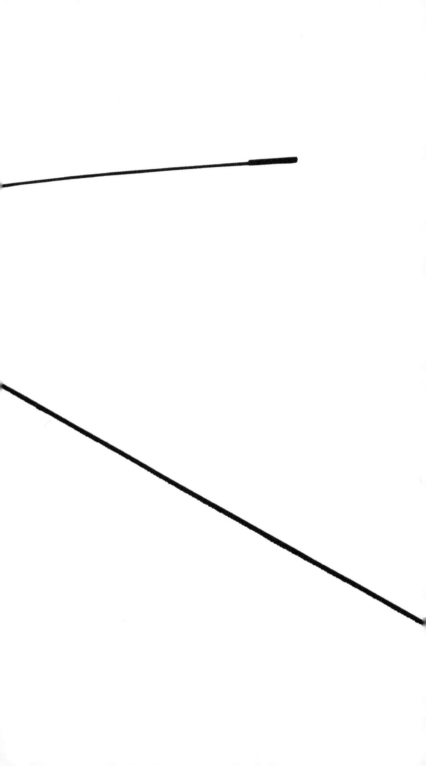

Preface

Preface

I wrote this book to provide aspiring as well as experienced entrepreneurs a concise guide to making the most of themselves and their ideas. It is a pocket bible for the high-potential changemaker, written to help business owners manage their focus and attention, realize their purpose, and achieve top performance.

#1nspiring sticks to the essentials while relying on a synthesis of the most accepted and implemented ideas used in business today. These include the Golden Circle (Simon Sinek), the Customer Development Process (Steve Blank), as well as ideas set forth in the books Value Proposition Design (Alexander Osterwalder) and The Lean Startup (Eric Ries).

After two decades of starting and running small businesses, in this book I share my experiences with you, future and experienced business owners and managers, to help you get inspired and fueled up for action. Whether you are a student or already active in your business career, this book is invaluable for everyone who aspires to start, build, and grow in business.

For your inspiration,
Bart Jenezon
bart@1nspiring.com

Introduction

Introduction

New methods to grow and improve businesses are required to launch and run successful enterprises. #1nspiring describes the basics of entrepreneurship, and provides tools and maps you can use to get going, to determine where you should focus, and to move from purpose to profit.

 #1nspiring offers guidance to entrepreneurs and small business owners. It provides an overview and a snapshot of the next steps to take to start, build, and grow your business. The book is intended to be a useful and inspiring resource to help you keep on the path to success. It provides clear and simple tools and offers readers a synthesis of the most accepted and implemented ideas used in business today.

The #1nspiring Method

This book walks you through the steps of starting, building, and growing your business using a three-stage business development model: Start, Build, Grow. The model enables you to develop your business step-by-step following these three essential stages, and breaking each down into three main components:

I. Start: Build your business on a strong foundation.
1. Idea (Purpose)
2. Mission/Vision (Value Creation)
3. Goals (Milestones)

II. Build: Activate and validate your business by finding paying customers.
4. Action (Game Plan)
5. Business (Product/Service)
6. Creation (Customer Development)

III. Grow: Grow the opportunity and expand your business.
7. People (Organization)
8. Planet (Market and Growth)
9. Profit (Finance)

"If we don't change direction,
we'll end up where we're going"
—Irwin Corey

1
- Idea
- Mission / vision
- Goals

2
- Action
- Business
- Creation

3
- People
- Planet
- Profit

A B C

This Book's Approach

Every element of your business offers choice, and each choice is connected to the next. By combining and tuning these parameters, you can "see" the opportunities of change and choice available to you and create clear outlines to bring them into being.

Start with your idea and purpose in order to define your mission, vision, and goals. Then put this into your business model through action, business, and customer creation; to reach a higher level of impact and performance with people all over the planet, you need to generate the necessary profit as a mutual benefit for all the shareholders and participants in the value chain. The diagram on the next page shows these steps in what I refer to in the book as "the inspiration canvas."

This practice can be used in several ways and at several points of your business development. You can use the inspiration canvas as your mind map, pitch deck, and business plan.When you need funding or just starting up you could use it as a business roadmap for your team, potential partners and possible investors.

Using the Inspiration Canvas

In this book, I take you through the inspiration canvas in order, from steps 1–9, as if you have just had an idea and thought, "Hey, I want to make a business out of that." But many people come to the inspiration canvas having already begun to investigate their business or with years of work on their idea behind them.

The #1nspiring method is a one that can be applied in many ways. In other words, the order in which you work through the inspiration canvas matters less than understanding how it reflects the ongoing process of building a successful entrepreneurial enterprise, in which you are often doing many things at once.

#1nspiring puts content into context. If you make a new version of the inspiration canvas each month or when you have another release or reach an important milestone, you will be thinking about where you are and keeping your focus where it needs to be. Whether you use the #1nspiring approach step-by-step, beginning from that moment when you have an idea for a business, or whether you use the inspiration canvas to improve a business already up and running, #1nspiring delivers clear and easy-to-follow steps to help you succeed.

Getting Started

If you are not using the inspiration canvas design printout provided with this book, it is the best to use a whiteboard or large piece of paper to create your own. Draw four lines into a big hashtag and you are ready to go. It's as simple as that.

The first time you use the inspiration canvas, write or sketch whatever comes to mind for each section—the first thought as far as where you would like your business to be or, if you're business is already established, where you think it is.

Do not write too much the first time. You are, in a sense, planning a trip, and right now you are simply determining if you will visit the ocean or the mountains, rather than a detailed itinerary.

During the second session, you add value and ideas to each section or focus in on one section. During the third session and in sessions that follow, you can prioritize and define your focus strategy. Use the inspiration canvas now to put in steps or outline a strategy for achieving what you have begun to articulate. You have decided to go to the mountains (or the moon). Great, how will you get there?

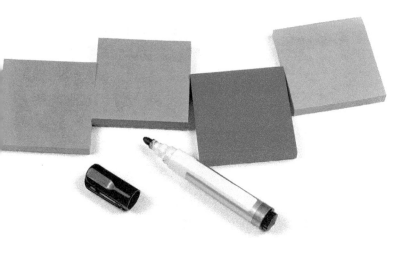

Idea
Purpose

Mission / Vision
Values

Goals
Milestones

A

Action
Game plan

B

Business
Product & services

C

Creation
Customers

People
Organization

Planet
Market

Profit
Finance

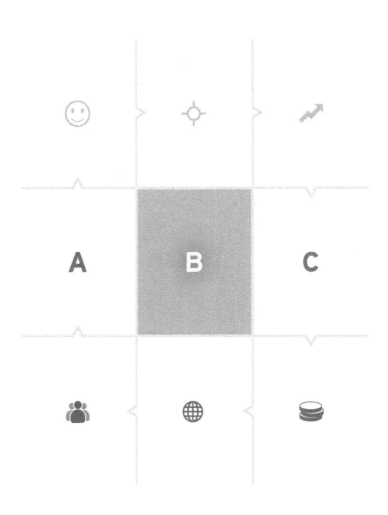

I. Start:

Foundation

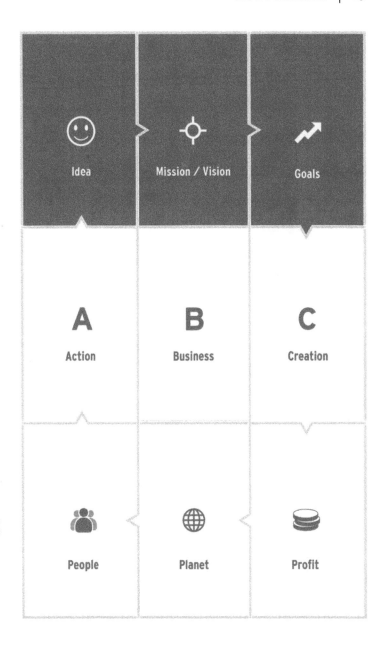

"Be the change
you want to see in the world"
—Mahatma Gandhi

I. Start: Foundation

This stage is the first section of the inspiration canvas and the foundation of your business. You have to stand up and go for it.

Your foundation has to contain the following elements:
- Idea (purpose)
- Mission/vision (value creation)
- Goals (milestones)

Ask yourself the following questions:
- What is my idea and purpose?
- What is the mission and vision?
- What do I hope to accomplish in 3–5 years?

Some additional questions to ask yourself:
- As I think about the long term, is it fun and exciting?
- Can I explain it to someone in less than a minute?
- Can I keep it simple?

This is the foundation on which to build your business.

Are you willing to take the next step?

1. Idea
(Purpose)

What is your idea and deeper meaning?

#introduction #idea #purpose

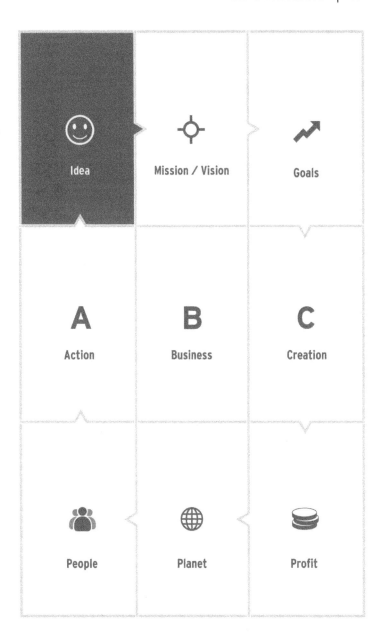

1. Idea

Your idea and purpose are the foundation of your business, life, and future. Write a description of the idea and purpose of the company or project.

- Purpose

Your purpose is more likely to draw in others who want to connect and contribute value to what you are doing. Purpose is not exactly the same as mission and vision.

Your purpose is the reason you work so hard or can't stop thinking about what needs to be done to get to the next step. It is a clear understanding of who you are and why you are here doing this.

- What is your idea all about?
- What is your purpose?

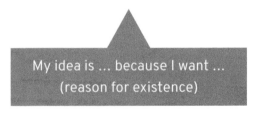

#why

It often takes months or even years to articulate and refine your purpose in the way you want, but doing so gives you a clear direction to follow, a base from which to work. That means that even if you think you know, when it comes to purpose, it is always worth asking why.

1.	Why?
2.	Why?
3.	Why?
4.	Why?
5.	Why?

5x

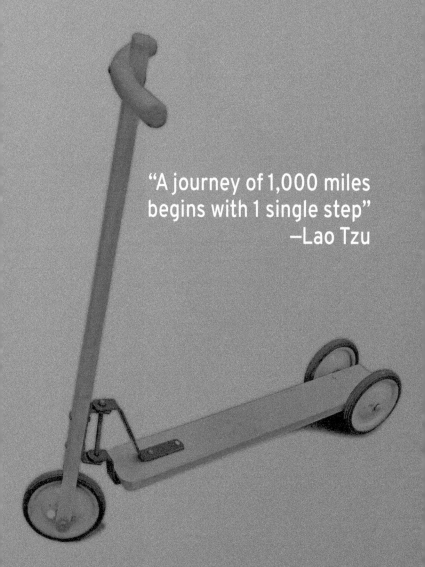

"A journey of 1,000 miles
begins with 1 single step"
—Lao Tzu

2. Mission/Vision (Values)

How will you make it happen?

#mission #vision #values

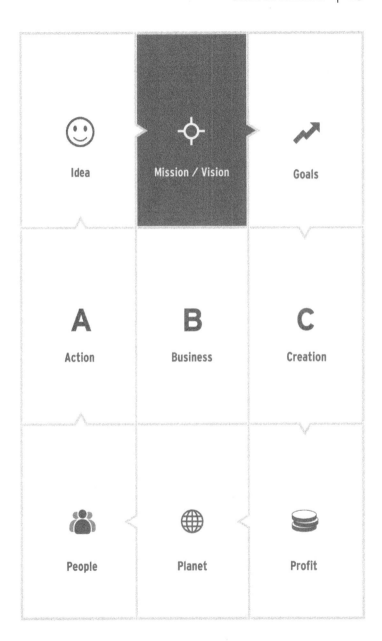

2. Mission/Vision

Mission and vision support your purpose. Mission and vision make visual the "how" and "what" questions you need to answer to make your "why" a reality. Your mission and vision will help you define how you will create value.

- Value creation

Some important questions underlying your mission and vision:
- What is your master plan and main challenge?
- What trends do you see arising in your field?

The mission and vision are the principles your company stands for and goes for..

- What is your mission and vision statement?
- What are your key values?

We stand for …
We go for …

#Mantra
Mantra for your business

Ideally, you would end up in this box with what Guy Kawasaki calls a "mantra" for your business. Here are some examples:

- Nike: Authentic, athletic performance.
- Coca-Cola: To refresh the world.
- Wendy's: Healthy fast food.

Your mantra sums up what your business or service does in a few beautiful words—not how it works, but what it actually does for customers.

What do you stand for and what are you going for?

"See the simplicity
in the complicated"
—Lao Tzu

Mission / Vision

3. Goals
(Milestones)

What are your goals?

#goals #milestones #bhag

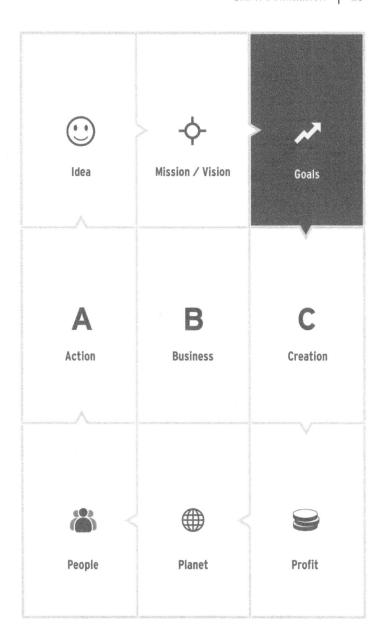

3. Goals

Now it is time to define what you would like to accomplish. What are the goals you have in mind?

- Goal setting

Setting goals is the perfect starting point for planning your business development and expected outcome. What is your schedule to approach them? Where do you plan to be in a month, a year, three years?

Let's start big:
- What is your dream and ambition?

Examples:
- We will be the leader in the industry.
- We will have our first paying customer.
- We will have ten new employees.

It helps to establish milestones.
- What are your goals?
- What are your milestones?

My milestones are 1 ... 2 ... 3 ...

Goals

S.M.A.R.T

Specific

Measurable

Achievable

Relevant

Time

#bhag

Think about your BHAG— Big, Hairy, Audacious Goal. It is a "super goal," a strategic business statement created to help you focus.

The term was coined by James Collins and Jerry Porras in their book, Built to Last: Successful Habits of Visionary Companies. It is a description of a single medium- to long-term goal (could be 10–30 years) to progress toward, an envisioned future and organization-wide goal that is audacious, likely to be externally questionable, but not regarded internally as impossible. Some examples:

- Neil Armstrong/John F. Kennedy: Land a man on the moon and return him safely to earth.
- Microsoft: A computer on every desk in every home.

A true BHAG is clear and compelling, serves as unifying focal point of effort, and acts as a clear catalyst for team spirit.

It has a clear finish line, so the organization can know when it has achieved the goal. People like to shoot for finish lines.

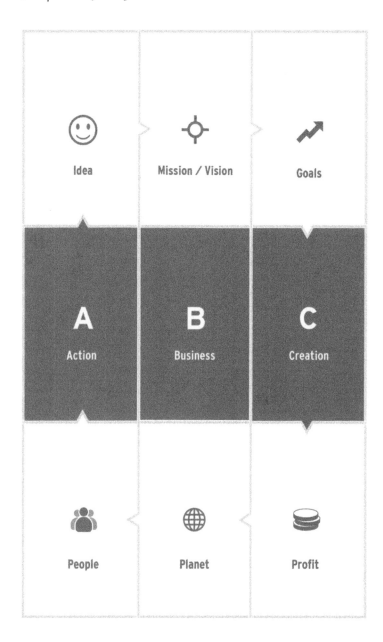

"The more experiments you make
the better"
—Ralph Waldo Emerson

II. Build:
Activation and Validation

II. Build: Activation and Validation

When you are ready you can look at how you will act. You will now test your ideas for improvement and sales.

This is the stage of activation or validation:
- A. Action (Game Plan)
- B. Business (Products and Services)
- C. Creation (Customer Development)

Ask yourself the following questions:
- What is my action plan to achieve all this?
- What is my business model, product, and service?
- How many customers do I have and will I gain?

The activation stage is where you will find validation and the right insights for your business. You have to find out what will work, yes or no, and adjust accordingly.

Action is the key.
It validates your business.
What are your next steps?

4. Action
(Game Plan)

What is your action plan?

#actions #marketing #tactics

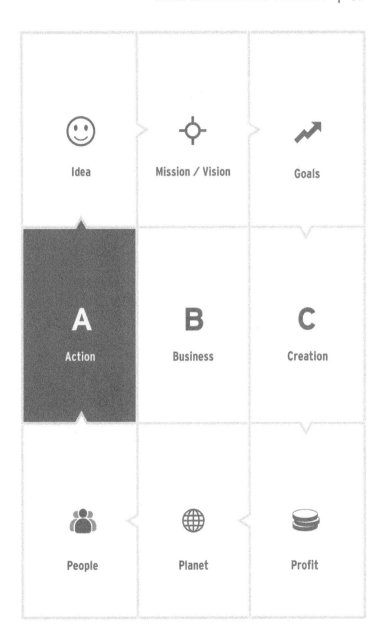

4. Action

Activation is about testing ideas to validate your business; therefore, we provide a number of ways to think about your game plan and which activities work for you.

What is your action game plan to achieve this business and idea?
- Game plan

You need to find out which activity will work and which will not. Pivot or persevere.

Some important questions to ask yourself about your action plan:
- Do I have a complete overview of all my activities?
- What is my marketing and sales plan?
- What are the next steps in product or business development?

Make a long list of anything that could improve and boost your business.
- What is my action plan?
- What are my next steps?

I (will) …
to activate my business.

#game-plan

#Product #Trademark #IPR #Logo #Design #Website
#Customer-surveys #Branding #Social media
#Marketing #Sales #Partnerships #SEO #SEA
#Freepublicity #Promotion #PR #Contracts
#Advertising #DM #Campaign #Terms

This is just a short list of some of the things that might be part of your action plan.

Because there is always a lot to do, set realistic goals in terms of schedule:
- As soon as possible.
- In the upcoming period/month.
- Before January.

Time for action!

Action is key!

5. Business
(Product/Service)

What is your product or service?

#product #service #business-model

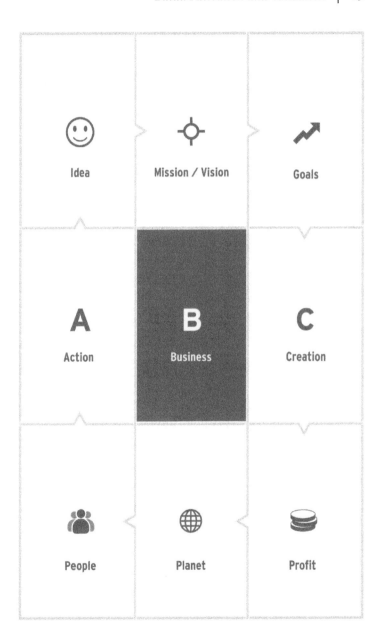

5. Business

Everything you do supports your business performance. The main focus has to be on running your business.

What product/service do you offer?
- Product/service

Some important questions to ask yourself about your business:
- What is my business offer?
- What is my primary business model?
- Do I have a secondary revenue stream and other income?

When you look at the activation stage, the business building block, is right in the middle of the matrix to give full focus and attention to.
- How do I create value?
- What is my product/service?
- What is the business model?

My product or service is ...

#business-model

- Advertising (television, ABC or NBC)
- License (franchise, Domino's or New York Pizza)
- Membership (club fee, Yoga Studio or Basic Fit)
- Provision (sales organization, Affiliate Marketing)
- Freemium and premium (publishers, New York Times)
- Subscription (monthly fee, Buffer or Zoom)
- Upfront (Chinese food or pizza delivery, Take-Away)
- Auction (market place, eBay or BVA-Auctions)
- Renting (Car rental, Hertz or Europe Car)
- Low-cost (Airline, Vueling or Transavia)

There are all kinds of business models and not all of them will work. Find your ideal business model by testing and validating it.

- What is my (possible) business model?

My business creates value with …

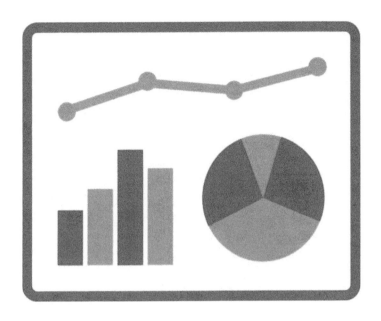

Build Your Business

Measure Your Performance

Learn from It

6. Creation
(Customer Development)

Who are your customers?

#clients #prospects #suspects

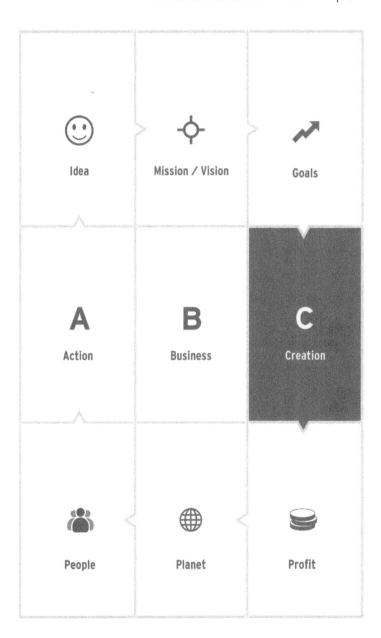

6. Creation

This section is about your customer creation and sales. All your effort leads to possible conversion, relationships, and customers.

What about your customer development?
- Customer development

Customer creation validates your business. You can measure your performance and learn from it. There are three key business drivers or deliverables in your sales flow at the end of the sales funnel:

1. Deals/clients:
   Contracts and new orders.
2. Prospects:
   Proposals for new business.
3. Suspects:
   Appointments and contact with potential customers.

Ask yourself:
- Who is my (potential) customer?
- How is the sales funnel looking, and what are the underlying sales figures?

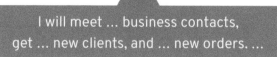

I will meet ... business contacts, get ... new clients, and ... new orders. ...

C   Creation

#salesfunnel

Key performance indicators:

- Clients (request for sales)
- Orders (request for information)
- Deals (contracts)
- Hot prospects (call or email)
- Prospects (new lead or contact)
- Proposals (offers)
- Super suspects (blue bird, tip)
- Suspects (data segmentation)
- Appointments (scheduled meetings)
- Contacts (data overall)

There are all kinds of performance indicators besides "hard core" sales, such as social media, customer contact, commercial inbounds, and customer care and satisfaction. It depends on what business you are in and what is relevant for you to monitor.

What is relevant to monitor in my business?

My key performance indicators are...

Always

Be

Closing

"If you can't fly then run,
If you can't run then walk,
If you can't walk then crawl,
But whatever you do,
You have to keep moving forward"
—Martin Luther King Jr.

III. Grow:
Co-Creation

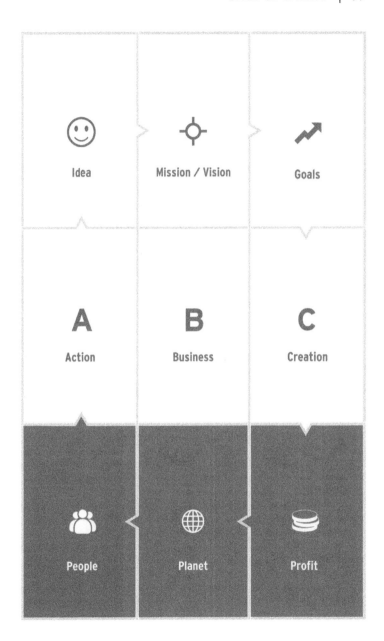

III. Grow: Co-Creation

If things go well in the activation stage, you are ready to think about further business development and growth. This stage is about scaling up your business, and sustaining and, if possible, multiplying it.

In this stage you think about:
- People (organization)
- Planet (market and growth)
- Profit (finance or funding)

Ask yourself the following questions:
- Who are the most important people?
- What are my growth markets?
- What is the profitability?

Business is always about the people and mutual benefits.

Businesses have to be sustainable by themselves.

Are you ready to grow?

7. People
(Organization)

Who is in your team?

#organization #team #partners

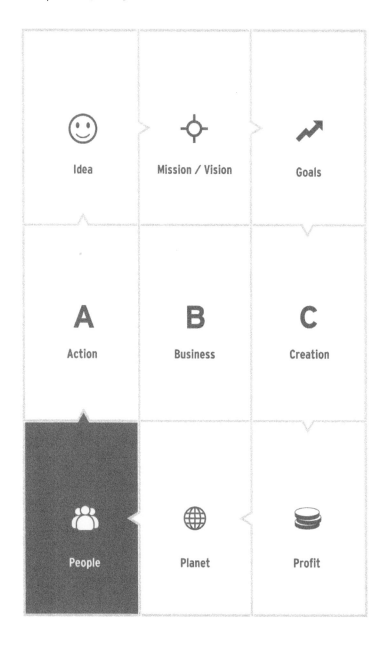

7. People

Your business is based on relationships.

What does your company look like?
- Organization

Some important questions underlying your organization:
- Who is involved in your business?
- Who are the key players in your team?
- What are their skills, roles and responsibilities?
- Who are your business partners and main suppliers?
- Who are your other stakeholders and participants?

The organizational structure must manage activities such as task allocation, coordination and supervision, anything and everything directed towards the achievements of organizational aims.
- Sketch out your team in an organizational chart.
- Make an overview of your business partners and suppliers.

My most important relationships are ...

#organization

List key management functions. Create a simple overview of functions in a small or medium-sized company. Maybe the company has or could have a board of advisors and/or supervisory board. They could be your formal or informal coach and business mentor. We invite our most important advisors into the board of inspiration.

- Write down the key people of your organization and their specific role and responsibility.
- Make a drawing of your organization with this organizational chart and structure.

What does your organization look like?

 **People**

"Growth is never by
mere chance;
it is the result of
forces working together"
—James Cash Penney

8. Planet
(Market and Growth)

What is your (growth) strategy?

#market #strategy #growth

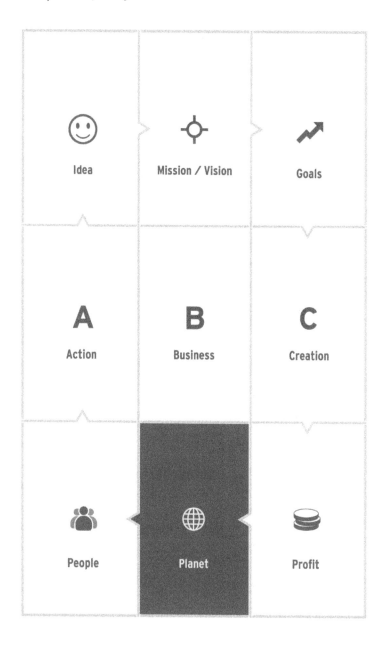

8. Planet

Time to get an overview of all the facts and figures of your (potential) customers and market share.

What is your market size?
- Market and growth

Ask yourself:
- What is my primary target group and what is my secondary market?
- Do I have other specific segmentations and/or alternative (new) business opportunities?
- Are my customers easy or difficult to attract?

Detailed information about your market segmentation:
- What are my (potential) markets?
- What is my target market?

My primary market is ...

#market-segmentation

Customer segmentation is the practice of dividing a customer base into groups. Customer segmentation relies on identifying "key differentiators," information such as:

Demographics
#age #gender #familysize #income #education

Geographics
#city #work #country

Psychographic
#socialclass #lifestyle

Behavioral
#spending #consumption #usage

Branches
Financial services, Business services, Industrial production, Government, Creative industries, Logistics, Energy, IT/ICT, Healthcare, Education, Wholesale and Retail, Hospitality

- How can I define segmentation for further focusing?

My focus is ... and will be ... in the future

Planet

9. Profit
(Finance)

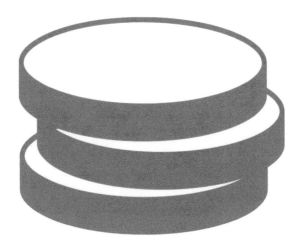

What about the financials?

#finance #profit-loss #investments

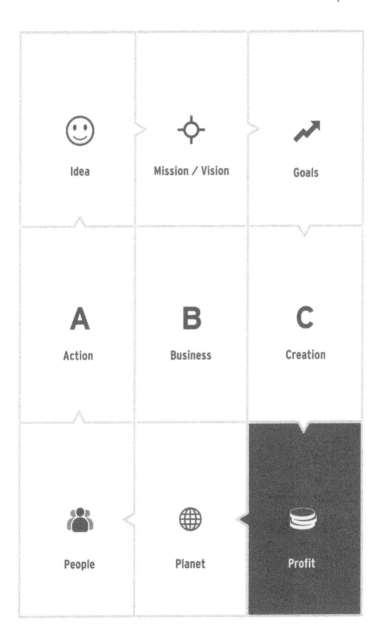

9. Profit

Facts and figures about the company or business project.

What financial statements could you make?

- Finance

Statement about the profitability and cash flow.

- Profit and loss statement
- Investments
- Cash flow statement

What money needs do I have (if any)?

- Short term
- Mid term
- Long term

- What are the prospective sources for revenue?
- What are all my costs and specifications?

My (possible) turnover will be ...

#profit and loss

<u>Revenues</u>

Net sales

Interest income

Other gains   _____

Total revenues   Total net sales

<u>Operating expenses</u>

Costs of goods sold

Personnel

Housing

IT and Telecom

Marketing

Sales

Travel

Legal and accountancy

Other

Total

Interest (paid)

Depreciation (fixed assets)

Total result

Profit

"By three methods
we may learn wisdom:
First, by reflection,
which is noblest;
Second, by imitation,
which is easiest;
And third by experience,
which is the bitterest."
—Confucius

Thank You & Call to Action

Thank you for taking the time to read this book.

Now you are ready to move forward and benefit from it!

You are always welcome to share your business ideas or thoughts about this book.

Feel free to join the #1nspiring platform,
https://join.1nspiring.com

Participate in the #1nspiring community,
https://www.linkedin.com/groups/3149968/

Download the canvas or drop me a line.

Keep on #1nspiring,
Bart Jenezon
bart@1nspiring.com
1nspiring.com

About the Author

Bart Jenezon (1973) is Chief Inspiration Officer and Founder of the 1nspiring Company, a company that supports people on their entrepreneurial journey by providing them with a simple format and clear logic to do what they have to do to succeed in business and life.

Appendix

Practice and Instruction

The first time you start practicing, you are writing and sketching just what comes up and what you have in mind.

In the second session, you add value and ideas to each section.

In the third session, you prioritize and define your focus.

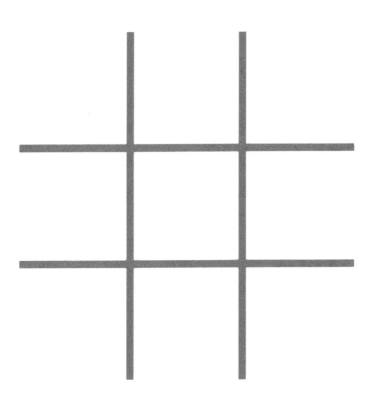

1. Idea
What is your idea and deeper meaning?
#introduction #idea #purpose

2. Mission/Vision
How will you make that happen?
#mission #vision #values

3. Goals
What are your goals?
#milestones #planning #bhag

4. Action plan
What is your action plan?
#actions #marketing #tactics

5. Business
What do you offer?
#product #service #business-model

6. Customer creation
Who are your customers?
#clients #prospects #values

7. People
Who is in your team?
#organization #team #partners

8. Planet
What is your primary market and growth?
#market #strategy #growth

9. Profit
What about the financials?
#finance #profitability #investments

Introduction

My idea is …

The purpose behind this idea is …

Mission statement

My mission is … and the vision is …

With these … underlying values …

Company goals

My company goals are …

The next milestones will be …

Marketing

My possible actions are …

The next actions will be …

Product/service

My product/service is …

And the business model is …

Sales

My (potential) customers are …

I have … customers, … suspects, … prospects

Organization

My key team members are …

The most important business partners are …

Market

My primary market is …

My growth market is …

Finance

My profit—and loss—is …

My need for investment is …

Green Soap Company

Green Soap Company produces and sells sustainable cleaning and personal care products. It was founded by Marcel Belt.

Start Case "Marcel's Green Soap"

Idea		Mission / Vision		Goals	
To start own soap company		Create a brand for cleaning products		European network	
⭐ 9/10	🖼 0	⭐ 10/10	🖼 2	⭐ 8/10	🖼 1
To clean up the place		Sustainable awareness		> 1.000 sales outlets	
⭐ 7/10	🖼 0	⭐ 8/10	🖼 1	⭐ 8/10	🖼 0
Green and mean		#natural #clean #fragrance		Scale-up company	
⭐ 0/10	🖼 0	⭐ 0/10	🖼 0	⭐ 0/10	🖼 0
	+		+		+

Action		Business		Customers	
Marketing & sales promotion		1 price, 4 products		Supermarkets	
⭐ 9/10	🖼 0	⭐ 9/10	🖼 0	⭐ 8/10	🖼 0
Build distribution network		4 products (all-cleaner, spray, dish & soap)		Healthy food stores	
⭐ 8/10	🖼 0	⭐ 8/10	🖼 0	⭐ 10/10	🖼 1
Build company and team		4 different fragrances		2.000 - 5.000 per week	
⭐ 0/10	🖼 0	⭐ 0/10	🖼 0	⭐ 0/10	🖼 0
	+		+		+

People		Planet		Profit	
Marcel Belt (founder)		Netherlands		350k to 1 MIO	
⭐ 9/10	🖼 0	⭐ 5.5/10	🖼 0	⭐ 0/10	🖼 0
Marketing & sales support		Benelux		Investment 200k - 500k	
⭐ 10/10	🖼 0	⭐ 8/10	🖼 0	⭐ 0/10	🖼 0
Production (the factory)		Germany, Ireland & UK		Margin 35%	
⭐ 8/10	🖼 0	⭐ 10/10	🖼 0	⭐ 0/10	🖼 0
	+		+		+

Marcel's Green Soap is inspired by Marcel's three daughters, the brand promise is one Marcel makes to his daughters for a cleaner and better future.

Showcase
"Green Soap Company"

Idea	Mission / Vision	Goals
Build environmentally friendly soap company	Sustainable cleaning & personal care products	International expansion
★ 1/10 1	★ 0/10 0	★ 0/10 0
Global brand for soap and detergent	Smells wonderful, works fantastically	Up to 10,000 outlets
★ 0/10 0	★ 0/10 0	★ 0/10 0
To clean up the place	And eco-friendly (100% recycled plastic)	60% offline, 40% online
★ 0/10 0	★ 0/10 0	★ 0/10 0
+	+	+

Action	Business	Customer
Acquisition & distribution	MGS: line of 62 products	Supermarkets
★ 0/10 0	★ 0/10 0	★ 0/10 0
Social media exposure	Driehoek: acquired from Unilever	Healthy food stores
★ 0/10 0	★ 0/10 0	★ 0/10 0
Sales promotion		Gardencenters & retail
★ 0/10 0		★ 0/10 0
+	+	+

People	Planet	Profit
Founder 1 FTE	Benelux	Sales 7.0 Mio
★ 0/10 0	★ 0/10 0	★ 0/10 0
Product/finance/logistics 3,5 FTE	Germany, Ireland and UK	CAGR 50%
★ 0/10 0	★ 0/10 0	★ 0/10 0
Marketing & sales 7 FTE	Scandinavia, China, Korea, US	Gross margin 30%
★ 0/10 0	★ 0/10 0	★ 0/10 0
+	+	+

"Ideas are easy.

Implementation is hard"
—Guy Kawasaki

Printed in the USA
CPSIA information can be obtained
at www.ICGtesting.com
JSHW072029140824
68134JS00045B/3849